DIRECT MAIL MAGIC

A Practical Guide To Effective Direct Mail Advertising

Charles Mallory

CRISP PUBLICATIONS, INC.
Los Altos, California

DIRECT MAIL MAGIC

A Practical Guide to Effective Direct Mail Advertising

Charles Mallory

CREDITS
Editor: **Elaine Brett**
Layout and Composition: **Interface Studio**
Cover Design: **Carol Harris**
Artwork: **Ralph Mapson**

Note to the Reader: This book is intended as a guide to give ideas about how to use direct mail advertising. Neither the author nor the publisher accepts any liability for losses from direct mail programs created as a result of information found herein.

Printed in the United States of America

English language Crisp books are distributed worldwide. Our major international distributors include:

CANADA: Reid Publishing Ltd., Box 69559—109 Thomas St., Oakville, Ontario Canada L6J 7R4. TEL: (416) 842-4428, FAX: (416) 842-9327

AUSTRALIA: Career Builders, P. O. Box 1051, Springwood, Brisbane, Queensland, Australia 4127. TEL: 841-1061, FAX: 841-1580

NEW ZEALAND: Career Builders, P. O. Box 571, Manurewa, Auckland, New Zealand. TEL: 266-5276, FAX: 266-4152

JAPAN: Phoenix Associates Co., Mizuho Bldg. 2-12-2, Kami Osaki, Shinagawa-Ku, Tokyo 141, Japan. TEL: 3-443-7231, FAX: 3-443-7640

Selected Crisp titles are also available in other languages. Contact International Rights Manager Tim Polk at (415) 949-4888 for more information.

Library of Congress Catalog Card Number 90-83478
Mallory, Charles
Direct Mail Magic
ISBN 1-56052-075-2

INTRODUCTION

When I did my first direct mail project, it was definitely done with a trial-and-error approach. In my job in public relations, I needed direct mail to support some telephone sales efforts. Because I was the department manager and worked directly for the CEO, I didn't have a supervisor to show me the way. I relied on many others where I worked, but I didn't even know what questions to ask. For instance, it didn't occur to me to think about the thickness of the response card until the U.S. Postal Service called and told me the paper on the response card was too thin. I didn't know I could save money by using carrier-route first class because I thought it was the same thing as presorted first class. I didn't have a budget to hire a direct mail consultant, although soon I wished I had.

I won't embarrass myself by mentioning the many mistakes on my first project. Fortunately, there were no post office penalities, and none of the pieces had to be reprinted. Most important, we got results that were good enough to encourage me to continue.

Years later, when I started my own firm, I had enough experience to offer direct mail consulting as part of my services. But I'll always remember that first overwhelming project.

Back when I was doing that project, I ran to three local library systems to find an easy-to-use direct mail guide for someone with little or no experience in the field. Though I found many good books about the theory of direct marketing, writing direct marketing copy, and similar topics, I never found an all-encompassing, easy-to-use guide. I checked *Books in Print* and found some more books. No easy-to use guide. So I wrote one.

If you have comments or suggestions for this book, please write me at:
Mallory Communications, P.O. Box 22403, Kansas City, MO 64113-2403.

Happy mailing!

Charles Mallory

Charles Mallory

DEDICATED TO JOYCE
May we "talk shop" forever.

ACKNOWLEDGEMENTS

Special thanks goes to the direct mail experts who allowed me to use portions of their work for this book: Joan Throckmorton, author of *Winning Direct Response Advertising*; Jack Schmid & Associates; and William Steinhardt of Steinhardt Direct. Also, thanks to Radio Advertising Bureau's *Sound Management* for letting me reproduce a brief article from the publication; Tension Envelope Corporation of Kansas City, which provided information for the section on mailing requirements; and Juanita Cartwright, mailing requirements clerk at the Shawnee Mission, Kansas, post office, for verifying mailing information.

The fine staff at Crisp Publications is much appreciated for their dedication and help. Thanks to Mike Crisp and Kathleen Barcos; also to Elaine Brett of Fritz/Brett Associates for a terrific editing job. I would be remiss if I didn't express my gratitude to author and speaker Twyla Dell, who first introduced me to Crisp Publications.

CONTENTS

Develop A Direct Mail Strategy

DIRECT MAIL—
DIRECT MARKETING—
MAIL ORDER—
WHAT'S THE DIFFERENCE?

Direct mail is one element of *direct marketing*. Direct marketing is a way to market products or services outside of the retail system. People who sell by telephone are doing direct marketing, but, of course, not direct mail. Direct marketing includes a variety of ways to sell products. Cable TV channels that sell products are using direct marketing, and so are magazine ads urging you to join a record club. *Mail order* is simply another name for direct mail.

Direct mail is certainly not an experimental form of advertising. According to an article in the *Kansas City Star*,* industry figures show that in 1989, 91.7 million Americans—virtually half of the adult population—shopped by direct mail.

NEARLY HALF OF THE ADULT POPULATION SHOPS BY DIRECT MAIL

**Kansas City Star Magazine*, March 25, 1990.

WHY AND HOW DOES IT WORK?

Direct mail provides a unique opportunity to target your customers, thus the word *direct*. It's true that you can advertise in a magazine that has a readership profile similar to your customer profile; however, even that audience cannot be segmented as accurately as direct mail.

Example:

An exclusive jewelry store wants to advertise its custom-made jewelry. The manager can choose between advertising in the city magazine, which is upscale and glamorous, and which has a reader profile that is close to the store's customers. It is obvious, however, that not every reader is a potential customer. Many readers do not have the median $75,000 income that is stated in the readership profile. Many may get the magazine just to see what concerts and other events are being held, while other readers only subscribe for "coffee table" effect and do not go through the whole magazine. And so on.

A better alternative for the jewelry store owner may be to acquire the mailing list from the magazine, create an attractive mailing piece, and then "purge" the list of the ZIP codes of neighborhoods with lower median incomes. The owner can even target only subscribers who live in the city's high-income ZIP codes, thus targeting an even higher-income market. Or, the store owner may elect to use both methods to market the custom jewelry as each message would tend to reinforce the other.

NO COMPETITION?

Some direct mail experts say that direct mail has no competition. Newspapers and magazines have many ads on various pages; TV has many sounds and images, all barking for the sale; and radio stations sandwich ad after ad so that they can offer "a 30-minute music sweep" of songs only. A direct mail piece, individually encased in its envelope, does not present readers with competing messages.

This is not the case. Most homes receive a number of pieces of direct mail every day. More importantly, direct mail is competing with something called *awaited first-class mail*: checks, letters from friends, ordered merchandise, and other items are pulled from the stack first with intense interest. Some people throw direct mail away unopened, but that number is relatively small. Despite the abundance of today's direct mail pieces, people are still concerned about the possibility of throwing away something valuable. Direct mail that is sent first class and/or looks like a personal letter, virtually becomes awaited mail, because the recipient wants to figure out who sent it. This interest may even allow direct mail to outdo awaited first-class mail in reader attention.

Direct mail has the distinct advantage of being a more personal selling experience than most other marketing forms. It is more personal to look at your personal four-color catalog of clothing in the comfort of your living room than it is to push through crowds at the mall. It is more effective to read about upcoming seminars while checking your organizer than it is to see the listing of seminars offered while glancing at the morning paper in the kitchen when your organizer is at your desk. And filling in the blanks on a response card is usually quicker and less annoying than calling a number that gives you a message every 30 seconds that says, "All customer service representatives are busy. Please continue holding. Your call will be answered in the order in which it was received."

KNOWING WHAT PEOPLE NEED AND WANT

Before you construct your offer, it's a good idea to examine human needs and wants. This will help you focus on creating an offer that is more likely to be a success.

HUMAN NEEDS AND WANTS

According to William Glasser, author of *Control Theory,* human beings have five needs:

- To survive and reproduce
- To belong
- To have power
- To have freedom
- To have fun

They also have ten "wants" (not in order of priority):

- To make and/or save money
- To save time
- To have tasks made easier or eliminated, especially routine chores
- To be comfortable
- To have good health
- To enjoy popularity/praise/style
- To be intelligent
- To gratify curiosity/satisfy appetite
- To possess beautiful or coveted things
- To be individual

CHECKLIST: EXACTLY WHAT DO I NEED TO DO?

For many businesses and entrepreneurs, a basic mailing is a good start. (If you need to do a catalog or multi-part mailing and have no experience, you should work with a direct mail consultant because of the complexity of the job.)

Here's a checklist of the steps for doing a basic direct mailing. Check each of them as you progress in your project. Look at the whole list before you use it. Depending on your particular circumstances, some of the components might be in slightly different order.

1. ☐ Understand what your customers and prospects want to buy.

2. ☐ Determine whether direct mail is really superior (for your type of business) to other marketing methods—public relations, space advertising, and telephone sales, for example—or whether it is at least worth testing.

3. ☐ Review other companies' direct mail pieces, especially those from competitors.

4. ☐ Determine a basic budget.

5. ☐ Construct your offer.

6. ☐ Set a schedule for completion. Set beginning and end dates for these steps:

   a. Developing the package and creative concept. Allow 2–8 weeks (more if you plan to hire outside writers and designers, or if the mailing piece is particularly complicated).
   b. Acquiring the mailing list. Allow 2–4 weeks.
   c. Printing the pieces. Allow 1–6 weeks.
   d. Preparation by the mailing house. Allow 1–4 weeks.
   e. Mailing date.

7. ☐ Meet with the mailing requirements clerk at the post office to determine whether you need a business reply number, what the mailing requirements are, and so on.

8. ☐ Determine the package components (formal letter with response card, for example) and mailing class (first class, third class, bulk mail, etc.).

9. ☐ Determine the number of people to whom you will mail.

10. ☐ Set a detailed budget.

CHECKLIST: WHAT DO I NEED TO DO? (Continued)

11. ☐ Review possible lists and choose one or more.
12. ☐ Write the copy and create the art, or hire copywriters and designers to do it.
13. ☐ Get printing bids (based on finished art and copy), and get bids from mailing services if needed. Double check with the post office on the size and weight of your finished piece—before it is printed.
14. ☐ Send the camera-ready artwork to printer; schedule with a mailing house if needed.
15. ☐ Plan a response mechanism procedure (temporary workers to fill orders, salespeople to take telephone inquiries, salespeople who will call on customers, etc.).
16. ☐ Send printed pieces to the mailing house. (It might be most efficient to have your printer do this.)
17. ☐ Begin tracking results as responses arrive.
18. ☐ After most responses are in, analyze the mailing and determine which components were successful or weak.
19. ☐ Add all respondents to your own in-house mailing list system.
20. ☐ Rent out your in-house list as soon as it becomes substantial and/or useful enough (a list broker can tell you).

WHICH ELEMENTS ARE THE MOST IMPORTANT?

There is a complex relationship between all the elements of a direct mail piece. The important elements are the lists used, the offer itself, the format of the mailing piece, the effectiveness of the copy, and the timing of the mailing. Based on manipulation of these elements, your response rate may vary as much as:

Lists used	1000%
Offer made	300%
Format used	150%
Copy used	50%
Timing of mailing	20% and more

Keep in mind that all of these elements work together. You can't ignore the timing because you have a fantastic list, even though the two items are very different in how they influence your results. And the most brilliant copy in the world can't sell products to the wrong list.

Information reprinted permission of J. Schmid & Associates, Inc., Shawnee Mission, KS.

TIMING YOUR MAILING

Knowing when to mail is very important. It might be based on your particular business. If you're going to send a mailing to announce a special event at your store, for instance, you might mail a month before the event.

You can devise a strategy for your mailing that will improve your results. According to J. Schmid and Associates, Inc., a leading direct marketing firm, tests show that some months are more responsive than others in direct mail. The table below shows the relative effectiveness of each month of the year. (January is the most effective month; February is 96% as effective, and so on.)

100 = Best time to mail	
January	100
February	96
March	71
April	72
May	72
June	67
July	73
August	87
September	79
October	90
November	81
December	79

Keep in mind that this does not preclude common sense. For example, you will not sell many toys at regular prices in January, because there are many reduced-price toy sales in the pre-Christmas season.

Catalog mailings are a special case; the best months to mail catalogs are September and October. For business-to-business mailings, January and September are the best months.

HOW YOU CAN USE DIRECT MAIL

Direct mail can be used to accomplish many marketing goals. Check the objectives that are applicable to your situation:

- ☐ To bring new customers into the store.
- ☐ To obtain repeat business from current customers.
- ☐ To identify leads for the field sales force.
- ☐ To identify leads for telephone sales follow-up.
- ☐ To do post-sales follow-up.
- ☐ To announce something new—a product or service, or an upgrade of a product or service.
- ☐ To support other advertising (TV/radio/newspaper/magazine advertising or public relations).

Think of other goals that would benefit your business:

- ☐ ____________________
- ☐ ____________________
- ☐ ____________________
- ☐ ____________________
- ☐ ____________________
- ☐ ____________________
- ☐ ____________________
- ☐ ____________________
- ☐ ____________________
- ☐ ____________________
- ☐ ____________________

CONSTRUCTING THE OFFER

Decide *what* you want the customer to do. That's your *offer*. Some basic offers are listed below. Develop an offer that is most suitable for your business. Don't be overly ambitious. If you own a retail store, a free demonstration is a perfectly fine offer. You can also combine offers. For example, you can offer a percentage-off sale for a limited time. This list will get you started with your own ideas; it does not represent all possible kinds of offers.

OFFERS

SALE

- A percentage off
- Time limit
- Seasonal
- Certain items or group of items (all men's clothing, shoes)
- Reason-why sale (overstock, slightly damaged)

FREE

- Gift with purchase
- Catalog
- Amount-off coupon/certificate
- Estimate
- Sample
- Delivery

GUARANTEE

- Money back
- Multiple amount of money back (double, triple, etc.)
- Free trial

You might be planning to use direct mail to invite customers to an open house. Is that an offer? In a sense. You are inviting others to see a new, renovated, or changed business. But the invitation can be enhanced by using one of the offers listed above.

EXAMPLES OF DIRECT MAIL OFFERS

Come to our open house—
and get a 25% discount
on all merchandise!

OPEN HOUSE

Free "Managing DOS" booklet just for viewing our new line of personal computers!

OPEN HOUSE

Sign up for free drawings—dinners for two and theater tickets.

Remember, it doesn't have to be simple if you don't want it to be. One innovative company started a hosiery club and customers carried membership cards. After each purchase of stockings, the card was punched, and after 12 purchases, the customer received a pair of stockings free. The original mailing piece included a card for all recipients, and the customer got the impression that the card made him a member of an exclusive club.

EXERCISE

Write some offer ideas for your business in the space provided below:

___

___

___

___

___

HOW TO SELECT AND RENT A MAILING LIST

Unless you have compiled your own mailing list, you will need to buy or rent one for your mailing. It is far more common to *rent* a list than to buy one. It is also far less expensive to rent an already-compiled list that represents potential buyers for your product or service than to create your own list from scratch. Your primary goal is to create a profitable return from a direct mailing.

Others have used and probably will use the same list you are renting, but if you've targeted the right list, this will not affect your response rate. Here are the steps to take in renting a list:

HOW

Find a list broker. A list broker finds lists and rents them to those who want them. Get recommendations of list brokers from other businesses that have sent direct mail, or check local directories. In telephone directories, look for the category "Mailing Lists."

If you would like to buy a mailing list for your exclusive use, check with a list broker.

Tip: Though list brokers will work with your marketing plan and recommend lists, you should do your own research. Nobody knows your business and your customers better than you do. Develop an approach to evaluate your customers—age, sex, income level, preferences, and other psychological and demographic factors. Review the *profile sheets* provided by list brokers. These sheets give information about names on the list in a variety of categories, and will help you select the lists that are right for your audience and offer.

You might also go to the library and check the book *Direct Mail List Rates and Data*, published by Standard Rate and Data Service. This volume lists the many direct mail lists available and might provide some new ideas as you search for the right list.

COST

Renting a list usually costs between $10 and $100 per thousand names, with additional minor costs for formatting or special sorting. Lists are provided in ZIP code order, since this is the preferred arrangement for mailing (and is required to receive U.S. Postal Service bulk rates). You may choose the option of ''special sorting,'' and have the names arranged or selected by region, profession, or other category.

You do not have to pay a broker's fee; he or she receives a commission from the list owner.

FORMAT

Determine in what form you want your mailing list. Here are three basic formats and how they are used. Check the one that is most appropriate for you.

____ *Mag tape*
A computer tape is used for large-number mailings (1,000+) when the address will be imprinted directly onto the printed material, or when you want to personalize a letter *and* print labels.

____ *Disks*
Microcomputer disks are useful when a mailing will be generated by your computer. Highly suitable when you rent a list for unlimited use rather than for a one-time mailing, but this is costly.

____ *Labels*
Use labels when you don't need the names and addresses printed on other materials. Labels can be purchased in Cheshire form—which means that the name/address block is positioned for special machines that cut, paste, and apply them to the mailing piece. Alternatively, they can be purchased in pressure-sensitive form for hand application to envelopes or other printed pieces. Determine whether your labels will be machine-applied or hand-applied.

HOW TO SELECT AND RENT A MAILING LIST (Continued)

TIME FRAME

Ask your broker how long it will take to receive your mailing list after you sign the contract. Generally, it takes two to three weeks from the time you inquire and sign the contract to when you receive the list, although with special arrangements an order can be rushed.

More Details About Getting a List

- Most list owners require a copy of what you will send as a direct mail piece. This is to ensure that the piece is in good taste or that closely competing organizations do not use the same lists. If you can print your piece before you choose the list, you'll be prepared. If not, send a draft of the copy that has been written along with a rough design of the piece. After your piece is printed, send a sample to the list owner, even if you've already used the list.
- Unless special arrangements are made, lists are rented for one-time use only. Lists are seeded with disguised names so that users that violate this rule will be discovered.
- You do not own a list when you rent it to mail your piece. If someone on the mailing list responds by sending you a card or replies in some way that gives you their name, address, and other information, you now own these names and can use them to compile your own mailing list.

TYPES OF LISTS

There are three types of lists; each kind has advantages and disadvantages.

	TYPE	ADVANTAGES	DISADVANTAGES
1.	**House List** A list of an organization's own customers.	Strong customer base; proven buyers.	Can be overused by owner; expensive to compile; takes time to build.
	Example: List of customers who have purchased major appliances from an appliance store, compiled from response or warranty cards sent back to the store. Response cards contain name, address, customer service information (satisfaction level), and other data.		
2.	**Response List** People who have taken action to be on a list by joining, subscribing, buying, calling, applying for credit.	Contains names of people who are interested in the product or service and who are more likely to respond to or read related mail; a relatively homogeneous group (likely to have common interests).	Selection of the right list is difficult because of numerous choices; list does not contain proven buyers.
	Examples: Subscribers to magazines and newspapers; members of social, political, professional, and other organizations; people who have applied for a credit card in the past six months; people who have purchased from a department store catalog in the past year.		
3.	**Compiled List** A universe of names, compiled from other lists or directories.	Good for blanket coverage of an area; less expensive.	Few or no segmentations based on market data; duplicated names can be as high as five percent. More likely to contain wrong addresses.
	Examples: Names of all adults living within a given ZIP code; names compiled from a city directory; names compiled from a telephone directory.		

TYPES OF LISTS (Continued)

Business-to-Business Lists

There are also business-to-business lists, which are used by businesses to market directly to specific kinds of other businesses. These can be targeted to particular positions in businesses—for example, to the presidents in a listing of advertising agencies. Or you could mail to all human resource directors at companies in the aerospace industry. If this is how your business operates, you'll want to use this type of list.

WHAT TO LOOK FOR IN A LIST

When you review possible lists, look for demographic and other characteristics that will give you a close match to your ideal market. List brokers can provide printed information that answers many of these essential questions. If you do not find a particular bit of information on the list description sheet, ask your broker if he can find the information.

Do not be dismayed if you cannot find answers to each and every one of these questions. For some questions, especially the *qualitative* ones, the information might not be available. All of the *quantitative* information should be there.

Questions to Ask	Sample Description Sheet
1. Name of list?	Current year home buyers in the state of Kansas
2. Total number of names?	56,000
3. Cost?	\$35/M (\$35 per 1,000 names)
4. How was list compiled?	From real estate agencies' sales reports
5. Date list compiled?	October (previous year)
6. What is the list profile?	
—Age	Average age 36
—Sex	51% male, 49% female
—Income	\$27,300 median family income
—Housing	
• Size of unit	Average 1200 sq. feet
• Length of residence	0 years
• Owner/renter	100% owners
• Home value	Average \$65,000
• Age of unit	Average 32 years
• Lot size	Average 3000 sq. ft.
—Buying style	
• Mail order buyer	Not available
• Purchase history	Not available
• Credit history	Available
• Special interests	Not available

WHAT TO LOOK FOR IN A LIST (Continued)

Questions to Ask:	Sample Description Sheet
—Family life cycle	
• Young singles	1%
• Newly married, no children	12%
• Married with children	81%
• Empty nest	5%
• Solitary survivor	1%

> *Note:* This profile is fictitious and was created for the purposes of this book. It does not present actual data.

ANALYZING THE LIST

Take a look at the sample description just given (pages 19–20). Let's say we are looking for a list for a mailing to find customers for a new statewide network of dental clinics.

Many aspects of the list look good. The cost, $35/M, or $35 per thousand, is inexpensive. It is recent enough—it contains homebuyers compiled in the past year. If we were planning to use a list to sell carpet cleaning services to people who had just bought carpeting, a better recency figure—such as all people who bought carpeting in the past *three months*—would be needed.

Details on home and lot size and buying style are acceptable and not of major concern. The income level is near the U.S. national average, and therefore all right. The length of residence is listed as zero because each buyer added to the list had just bought the home. The people on this list have bought a house within the past year and obviously are not likely to have moved away since they made the purchase; therefore, the accuracy rate should be high.

Since these are new homebuyers, the list will include some people who are new to the region in which they bought their home. They are likely to be interested in knowing about a new dentist on whom they can rely. And though everybody should go to the dentist, we know that children are a prime market—and 81% of the people on this list have children who live at home.

But *one important factor*: the list was compiled from real estate agencies, meaning that *those who rent, already own a home,* or *bought a house directly from the owner* are not included in this list. Perhaps this is not a problem—or it could mean the omission of thousands of higher-income, bigger-family, more recent names!

After you ask your broker for description sheets from several lists that might suit your needs, take your time in analyzing them. This requires reading the information—and then reading between the lines.

OTHER OPTIONS FOR FINDING LISTS

OPTION #1

You do not have to go to a list broker to get a list. Some business people choose to find the appropriate list through a directory or by recognizing a valuable list just from observation.

For instance, if you receive a catalog containing upscale women's apparel, and you are selling similar items, you can contact the catalog company and attempt to rent their list of customers who have purchased from the catalog.

It is even possible to circumvent the list-broker middleman and obtain a better deal. The most common commission paid to a list broker is 20%–25%. The commission is paid by the list owner to the broker, and it is standard practice for a list to cost the same whether it is rented from the organization or through a broker. Why? The organization accepts lower profit and pays the broker the commission when the list is rented because the broker did the work of finding a list renter.

Sometimes, if you approach the list owner directly, you can negotiate a discount that would normally be given to the list broker. Don't assume that you must be given a discount just because you do not use a broker; some organizations adhere to a cost-per-thousand that is non-negotiable.

OPTION #2

Many mailing houses offer full-service mailing. If you plan to use them for other services, such as printing, imprinting addresses, stuffing and sorting, mailing, and other services, they will also gladly serve as list broker. Get to know your account representative at such a company to assess the value of this approach. Make certain that the person working with you in selecting a list is knowledgeable about direct mail lists. Keep in mind that the organization is acting as a broker, so you will not be able to achieve the discount mentioned in Option #1 above.

To eliminate hassles, some businesses are going to full-service mailing houses for the entire program: generating the idea, copywriting and design, printing, finding a mailing list, and handling all aspects of mailing to the consumer. This might be suitable for you, but you will probably pay a higher rate because services (writing, designing, printing) are often contracted to freelancers and then marked up in price by the mailing house.

HOW DO YOU MERGE AND PURGE?

A term often used in direct mail is *merge and purge*. This is a computer-run operation used when you mail to more than one list in a single mailing. Two or more lists can be *merged* and then duplicate names are *purged* from the list. If you use a list brokers request the combined list to be provided this way (there may be an added charge for the service).

Example

An entrepreneur who has a one-person operation providing career consulting and resumé writing decides to do a mailing to three lists:

- Graduates (current year and the past two years) of a local college—394 names.
- Subscribers to a local business magazine—12,400 names.
- Members of the Advertising and Public Relations Club—692 names. (This is the entrepreneur's experimental list; she knows that job-hopping is more prevalent in these businesses.)

The three lists are merged, then purged. Let's say there are 230 names who are on more than one list. That eliminates 230 pieces of mail, because those 230 will get *one* copy of the piece instead of two or three. Merging and purging the three lists not only saves the entrepreneur a few bucks, but more importantly, the mailing is more effective to those 230 people because they aren't annoyed by getting two or three copies of the same piece.

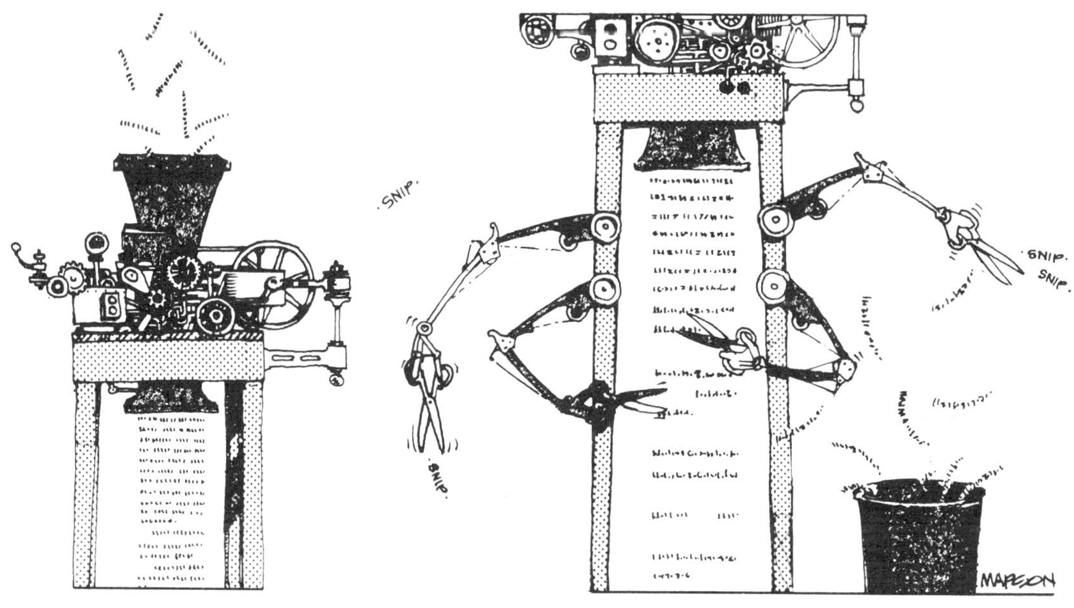

MERGE *MERGE AND PURGE*

BUDGETING YOUR DIRECT MAIL CAMPAIGN

First-time direct mailers often make the mistake of not thoroughly budgeting all the costs of a direct mail campaign, and then looking at whether the campaign will be profitable at an acceptable rate. Like any other marketing effort, direct mail must be analyzed on the basis of *return on investment* (ROI).

You begin by determining what an appropriate return on investment is for your company. Depending on what kind of business you are in and what your normal ROI is, this can range from as low as 5% to as high as 30%. If you usually get an ROI of 20% in your business, you should get at least that from a direct mail campaign; if your profit projections for a direct mail campaign fall below that, you should probably invest your money in some other marketing effort that can be counted on to return 20%.

Here is a basic list of the costs that you should include in your budget:

Designing the Mailing Piece
- Creative management
- Copywriting
- Design and production

Mailing Costs
- Bulk mail permit, if appropriate
- Cost per piece to mail first class or at bulk rates
- Mailing house costs to attach labels, sort for the post office, and deliver to the post office
- Business reply permit
- Cost per response for using business reply envelopes or cards

Printing Costs
- Cost of paper, envelopes, and other materials
- Per-piece cost to print each part of the package
- Delivery charges to deliver to mailing house

List Costs
- Total number of names you will use, times the cost per thousand
- Additional charges for special sorts or for pressure-sensitive labels

Testing Costs
- Cost for randomly selected names
- Cost for test pieces specially printed at low volume
- Cost for mailing house to follow test design

Consulting Costs
- Cost for consulting time to advise on the offer, packaging, list selection, test design, and any other elements of the direct mail plan

When your budget is complete and all costs have been identified, you still need to know what your probable profitability is. This cannot be determined without some knowledge of what the rate of return on the mailing piece is likely to be. You must test the list, and perhaps other elements of the direct mail package, in order to determine the rate of return.

TESTING THE LIST AND YOUR OFFER

Even when lists appear to have all the right characteristics to bring in a high rate of responses, they sometimes fail to do so. Unless a list is very small—less than 2000—it is important to test it to make sure you will have a rate of return that meets your profitability goals. It is recommended that you test at least 1,000 randomly selected names from a list before you rent the whole list.

You may also want to test the offer itself, or the packaging of the offer. Testing elements of a mailing is a very sophisticated process because the elements may interact in unexpected ways, but testing can make the difference between making or losing significant amounts of money. The larger the investment you are making, the more important it is to test the lists and other elements before you start mailing to thousands of people. If you are undertaking a large investment, you should consult a direct mail expert to help you design your testing process.

Here is a simple test design. Suppose you are a direct mail office supply company, and you want to attract new customers with an offer for microcomputer disks. You have two lists that appear appropriate—18,000 corporate subscribers to an office management journal, and a list of 10,000 corporate buyers. You are hesitating between using one or both of the lists, and you are also considering making your offer two different ways:

- Offer A: 100 disks for the amazing price of 89 cents each!
- Offer B: Buy three packs of 25 disks for $89, get a fourth pack free!

Notice that the buyer pays the same amount in either case; however, many people are attracted to offers that give them something free, and you want to know whether this approach will give you a better return.

TESTING THE LIST AND YOUR OFFER (Continued)

You can actually test both elements—the two offers and the two lists—using only 1,000 names. This is done with a test design called *matrix testing*. Here's how it works. You would create two test pieces, one making Offer A, and one making Offer B. Print 500 copies of each piece. Order 500 randomly selected names from each list. The response cards are coded in some way so that you will be able to tell which mailing list each respondent was on. The 1,000 pieces are then mailed as shown in the matrix below:

	Offer A	**Offer B**
List A	250 names	250 names
List B	250 names	250 names

As the responses come in, they are tallied in these four categories, then the rows and columns are added together. Suppose the responses look like this:

	Offer A	**Offer B**	**TOTALS**
List A	2 (.8%)	5 (2.0%)	7 (1.4%)
List B	3 (1.2%)	7 (2.8%)	10 (2.0%)
TOTAL	5 (1.0%)	12 (2.4%)	

Your suspicion that people prefer an offer of something free is confirmed; you decide to use Offer B. You should probably use List B for sure, and whether or not you use List A depends on what you learn when you work on your budget and ROI.

A matrix test allows you to get more information from just a few names. More than two elements can be tested in a more elaborate matrix—but you need an expert to design such a test.

Although such a test does not predict with complete precision what your final return will be, it is close enough so that you can construct your projected return on investment with confidence.

GETTING AN EARLY PREDICTION OF RESPONSE RATE

If you are on a tight schedule—or just dying to know whether your test shows that your offer and lists were successful—you can cut down on the time needed to predict your response rate by using the principle of the bell curve. You probably remember teachers who graded ''on the curve.'' The number of responses received in the mail or on the phone, like test scores, tend to fall into a bell-shaped curve. For example, here is a vastly oversimplified example of a response per day count on a mailing of 1,000, beginning with the day the first response was received:

		Cumulative responses
Day 1	1	1
Day 2	0	1
Day 3	2	3
Day 4	4	7
Day 5	6	13
Day 6	5	18
Day 7	3	21
Day 8	2	23
Day 9	0	23
Day 10	0	23
Day 11	1	24

If you plotted this on a graph, it would look like this:

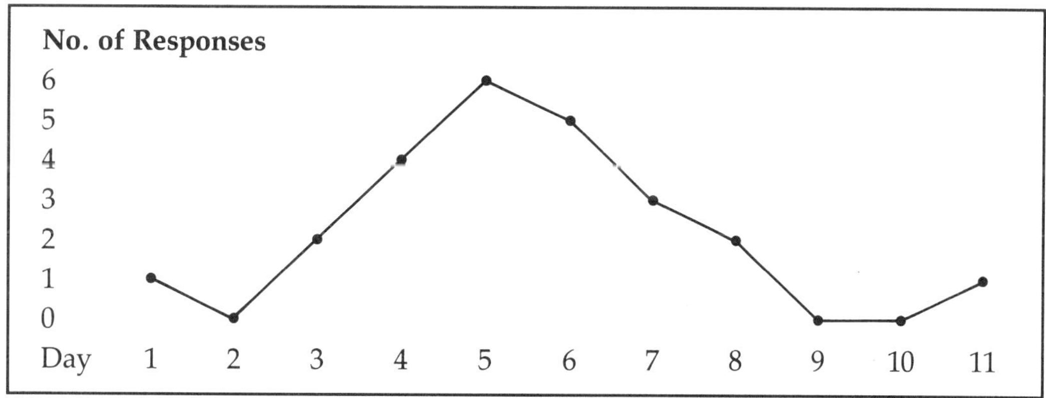

You can see that there is a more or less halfway point at which the number of responses begins to decline. You can use this point to predict the final rate of response. For example, you notice that at Day 6, the rate begins to decline, and you guess that 50% of the responses are now in, or rather that they were in by Day 5. If the final count is twice the cumulative count for Day 5, 26 responses will be received, for a response rate of 2.6%. This is not a completely accurate predictor—in our example, the final count was 24, for a 2.4% response rate. But it is an indicator that can be useful—at least you know the rate is very unlikely to be below 1% or over 3%. As you get more experience with doing tests in your market, you will be able to predict from the curve with increasing accuracy.

CALCULATING YOUR RETURN ON INVESTMENT

With a detailed budget and a proposed return rate, you are ready to project your probable ROI. This is a perfect exercise for a spreadsheet program on a computer. Spreadsheets make it easy to ask "What if...?" types of questions so that you can immediately see the effect of changing some element of the package. For example, if your projection is disappointing, you might see whether the ROI becomes satisfactory if you decide to have respondents use their own stamps rather than your paying the postal charges for a prepaid response card. You would need to adjust your response rate downward since people are somewhat more likely to respond if they don't have to provide a stamp.

Let's continue the example of the disks offer. You decide to use only List B. Your test indicates a rate of return between 2.8% (Offer B, List B) and 2.4% (all Offer B). Here is a typical ROI analysis:

Direct Mail Costs

Number to be mailed: 10,000	
Cost per piece (printing, materials)	$ .57
Mailing costs per piece (postage, mailing house)	$ .42
Cost of list ($45/M, or $.045 each)	$ .045
TOTAL COST PER PIECE	$1.035
Cost per piece × 10,000	$10,350
One-time costs (postal permits, creative services, testing, consulting)	$ 9,450
TOTAL COSTS	$19,800

Projected Income

Average order amount	$100	
Income at 2.4% return	$24,000	(240 × 100)
Income at 2.8% return	$28,000	(280 × 100)

Return on Investment

At 2.4%	$24,000 – $19,800 costs	equals $4,200
ROI	21.2%	($4200 / $19,800)
At 2.8%	$28,000 – $19,800 costs	equals $8,200
ROI	41.4%	($8200 / $19,800)

If your business should get at least a 20% ROI, this is a promising analysis—you can predict with some confidence that your ROI will be at least 21.2%, and probably higher.

Not all analyses turn out so well. It is better to cancel a campaign after a test that indicates that the concept will not work. Many inexperienced direct-mailers do not do the essential testing, budgeting, and ROI projections. If a campaign is not well constructed, you can actually lose more money with every additional piece you mail—not a good way to do business!

CHOOSING A FORMAT

A wide variety of formats are possible. Just take a look at some of the direct mail offers you've received and you'll see what I mean. There are black-and-white pieces printed on inexpensive paper, and expensive, four-color, glossy pieces; there are simple letter-in-envelope pieces and fold-out brochures. There are many options for packaging your offer.

A simple package might be a good idea if this is your first venture in direct mail. Remember, though, that the main criteria is the piece's ability to produce results. A hairstyling salon that wants to attract customers by announcing that they've just hired a new, popular stylist could simply send an attractive four-color postcard with the news; that might be all the ''package'' that is needed. A basic package might include a letter, some mechanism for a response, and, if necessary, a brochure.

LETTER

The letter introduces your product or service to the recipient, and can be printed on letterhead, special stationery just for this mailing, or plain paper.

OUTER ENVELOPE

This will contain all the pieces within; a blurb can be printed on the outside, and a return address might also be on the envelope.

RESPONSE MECHANISM

This can be a tear-off portion of the letter (perhaps perforated by the printer), a separate card, or other device.

BROCHURE

Though a brochure is not a must, many direct mail pieces contain some piece to accompany the letter. It more fully describes and demonstrates your product or service.

BUSINESS REPLY ENVELOPE

If your response mechanism is not a business reply card (which is self-mailing), a business reply envelope further pushes the recipient to answer.

CHOOSING A FORMAT (Continued)

Sometimes it's *how* you treat the particular piece that determines the format. A basic package can be hard-sell, containing an outer envelope filled with blurbs (''YOU might be the next big winner in the Super Sweepstakes!'') with busy, wealth-promising artwork on the inner pieces. You can use a *lift letter*, which is often seen in magazine-subscription approaches that have a ''Yes, I'll subscribe'' envelope and a ''No'' envelope. Sticking out of the ''No'' envelope is a lift letter that says, ''Please don't say no—not now!''

A mailing piece can be highly personalized, especially when laser printing is used. Sometimes a piece is printed with a line left blank; than that line is lasered in. That's why some sweepstakes pieces look like this:

> Just imagine, MR. DOE...all your friends on ELM STREET
> will envy you as you cruise down the street
> ***in your new car!***

A good rule of thumb is that the fancier a package is, the more it costs. Determine what product or service your customers and prospects want to buy and how that mailing piece should sell to them. This is a common-sense logic. If you own a store that sells gourmet cooking items and has classes in gourmet cooking, the potential customers need to see mouth-watering color photos of food; hard-sell copy in black-and-white is the wrong approach. Or for another example: if you're mailing to your own list of previous customers, don't waste your money with lasered-in names and addresses to personalize the letter.

A RESPONSE CARD SHORTCUT

To increase effectiveness and accuracy in your mailings, it's a good idea to use a label or mag tape address on the response card or form itself. This address can be coded to instantly identify which list the name was on, which helps you track your results accurately. This technique also reduces the amount of the time needed for your customer or prospect to fill in an order form, since the name and address are already there.

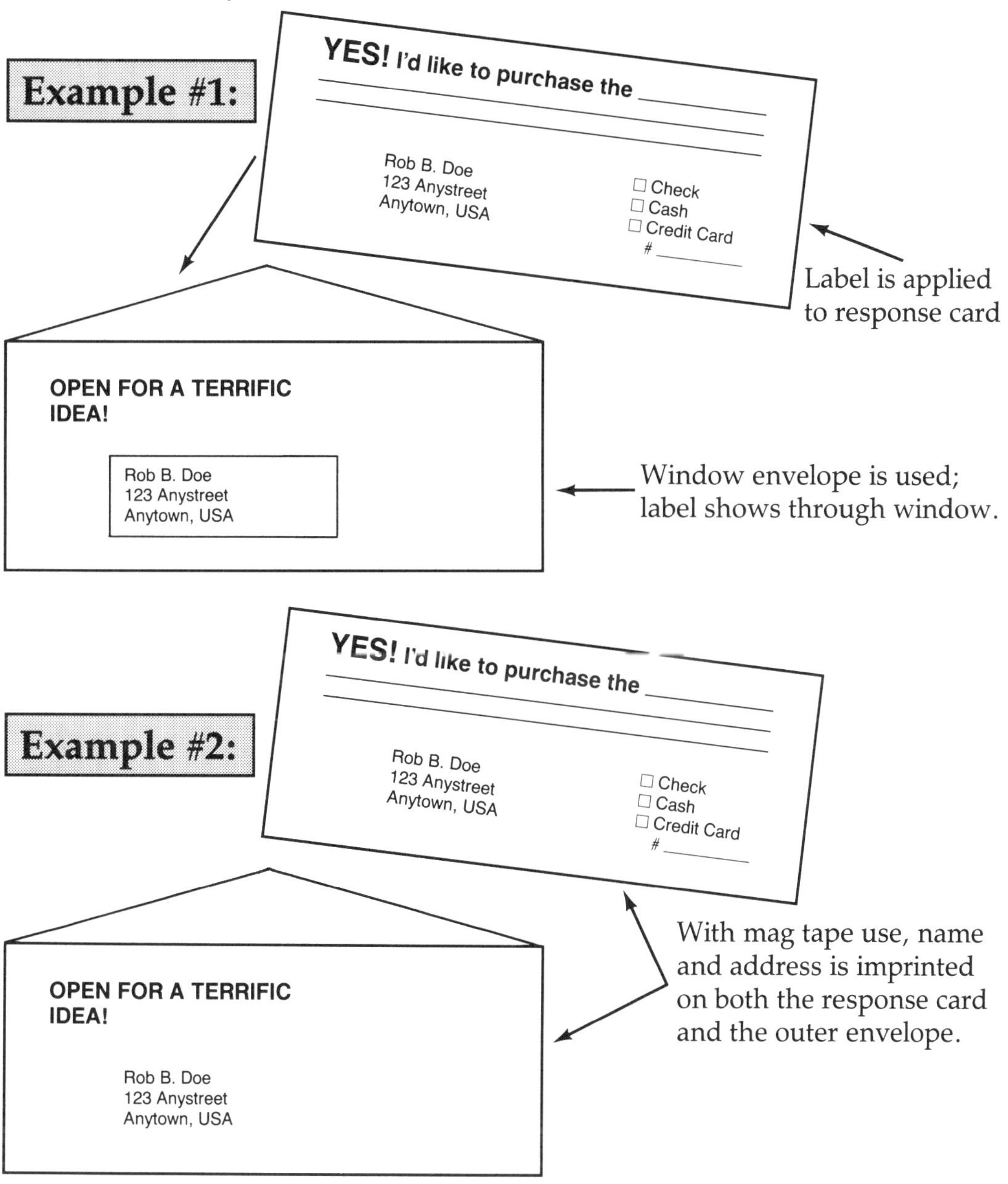

WHERE DO I DRAW THE LINE?

It's confusing to figure out how expensively or cheaply to produce a direct mail piece. You would think that top-of-the-line paper, an expensive, well-designed envelope, and copy written by an expensive professional would always do better than an inexpensive mailing that you and your own staff might create. The assumptions do not always hold true. Sometimes an expensive direct mail piece is less effective than a more cheaply produced one.

Generally, envelopes printed with a bulk rate permit get a better response than postage-metered envelopes; a heavier, costlier letterhead gives a better impression and may create more responses than inexpensive paper; a four-color brochure usually draws more responses than a two-color brochure. Even when these rules of thumb are true in some markets, they may not work in yours. Some of the most profitable pieces ever used are design horrors—busy and inelegant. You can test each design of course, but this is expensive. Common sense and market knowledge make a big difference.

Your goal is to create the highest response possible within your budget. When making your plans, strike a balance between economical and luxurious, unless your product or service strictly calls for one or the other. A classy jewelry store needs an expensive package to create an appropriate image; a nonprofit community organization might not want to have a package that is too slick—it might make contributors think they're giving donations to the organization's printer! Some nonprofit organizations get their direct mail materials donated and state so on the package.

Direct mail is the business of testing. Here's a rule to live by that will help you know when to draw the line:

RULE # 1, 2, 3 through Infinity: Keep accurate and detailed records of your direct mail programs, including a record of all elements and costs, a copy of the complete package, and final rates of return and ROI. Learn what works and what doesn't for your organization. Once you have the numbers, analyze them to plan your next move.

Develop Your Creative Approach

PUTTING OFFER, PACKAGE, AND COPY TOGETHER

Once you've determined what your offer will be and how you will package it, it's time to write the copy. Even if you hire a writer, suggest that he or she use the Creative Strategy Outline shown in the example below. This is the genesis of the copy and graphic design that will shape the final direct mail piece. The Creative Strategy Outline was created by Joan Throckmorton, author of *Winning Direct Response Advertising*.

Creative Strategy Outline

Title of Job:	*Vital Woman* magazine, the first comprehensive magazine devoted to women's health and fitness.
Competition:	None. This is the first such publication.
Market:	Active, busy women between the ages of 18 and 34. (Women who have shown an interest in health and fitness publications, exercise book buyers, etc.)
Offer:	Charter Offer, 1 year for $15; full money-back guarantee. Premium ("Answers to 24 of Women's Most Troublesome Health Questions").
Hypothesis:	Women want to be better informed about their health and general well-being so they can take control of their lives, make wiser decisions, and improve their relationships with their doctors. This enables them to avoid risk and worry because they can understand and solve or prevent many problems and live a more healthy life.
Copy/Platform Benefits:	*Vital Woman*, the first magazine devoted to women's health and fitness, will enable you to take more responsibility for your own health —via expert medical advice on health and fitness. —via a better understanding of women's health and fitness problems. —via a natural approach to health. The result will be —a better relationship with your doctor. —a healthier, happier life.

CREATIVE STRATEGY OUTLINE (Continued)

First Copy Statement:	You are the primary diagnostician. Let *Vital Woman* help make sure that the *one* person who can take care of you best does a good job. —Take charge of your own health with *Vital Woman.* —Put your health in the best hands—your own. —Don't waste time and money on unnecessary doctor visits.
Second Copy Statement:	Make sure your doctor takes you seriously. (Why should you feel neurotic every time you feel sick?)
Third Copy Statement:	Join a round table of foremost women's physicians every month. Sit down and listen. Ask questions.
Secondary Benefits/Features:	—Sound information on natural healing (keep medicine and drugs to a minimum) —Pros and cons of major women's health issues —Reader Q's and A's —Medically approved diets and exercise —Emotional and interpersonal advice —10 pages of color, many illustrations in every issue —Use deadline for offer —List full advisory board on first page of letter. —Make the spokesperson a credible woman (female publisher).
Format:	Direct mail package/Third-class mail Outer envelope 4-page letter (2-color) Brochure (4-color) Order card 1-page lift letter

Now that you've seen an example, create your own Creative Strategy Outline.

CREATIVE STRATEGY OUTLINE

Title of Job: ______________________________

____

Competition: ______________________________

____

Market: ______________________________

____

Offer: ______________________________

____

Hypothesis: ______________________________

____

Copy Platform/Benefits: ______________________________

____

First Copy Statement: ______________________________

____

Second Copy Statement: ______________________________

____

Third Copy Statement: ______________________________

____

Secondary Benefits/Features: ______________________________

____

Recommendations: ______________________________

____

Format: ______________________________

____

Reprinted with permission from *Winning Direct Response Advertising* by Joan Throckmorton; Prentice Hall, 1986.

WRITING THE COPY

After developing your Creative Strategy Outline, move on to actually writing the piece. Keep in mind the copy statements you wrote in your creative strategy. Don't create in a vacuum. Allow others, particularly expert friends and colleagues, to review your direct mail copy.

If you're hiring a writer, feel free to suggest that he or she use this outline approach. It's a good idea to find a free-lance copywriter who has previously written direct mail pieces. The stars in the business are somewhat expensive for small businesses, but there are many others who are very good and affordable.

There are many ways to find free-lance direct mail copywriters if you don't have contacts through business associates:

- Contact the local chapter of the Direct Marketing Association (DMA).
- Contact the local chapter of IABC (International Association of Business Communicators).
- Contact the local advertising club.
- Check the Yellow Pages under Advertising—Direct Mail or Writers.

Talk with candidates about their previous experience and what pieces they wrote that worked well. Review each writer's portfolio. The sections that follow are useful if you choose to write the copy yourself.

TEN-POINT A-B-C CHECKLIST

Here's an automatic outline you can use when you create your direct mail copy. By placing these proven elements in your direct mail piece, you greatly increase your chance for success. (Useful words and examples follow this checklist.)

Ten-Point A-B-C Checklist For Dynamic Direct-Mail Copy

1. ATTAIN ATTENTION	6. FEATURE SPECIAL DETAILS
2. BANG OUT BENEFITS	7. GILD WITH VALUES
3. CREATE VERBAL PICTURES	8. HONOR CLAIMS WITH MONEY-BACK GUARANTEES (SATISFACTION)
4. DESCRIBE SUCCESS INCIDENT	9. INJECT ACTION IN READER
5. ENDORSE WITH TESTIMONIALS	10. JELL WITH POST-SCRIPT

Reprinted with permission of William Steinhardt, Steinhardt Direct, Shawnee Mission, KS.

14 ATTENTION-GETTING APPROACHES

Start your direct mail copy by grabbing the reader. It is difficult to get the reader to open the mail; make sure the reader picks up the mailing piece and reads through it. Here are several useful approaches:

APPROACH	SAMPLE	WHEN TO USE
1. *Invite*	I'd like to invite you to sit down with one of the world's greatest books.	To sell a high-resistance item or to sell to a high-resistance audience (for example, persons with income $100,000+, who are likely to be busy achievers).
2. *Quote*	"The great mystery of time, were there no other; the illimitable, silent, never-resting thing called time, rolling, rushing on, swift, silent, like an all-embracing tide." —Thomas Carlyle.	To evoke emotion; to establish environment; to announce or to say something with authority.
3. *Give testimonial*	"Our sales increased fifteen percent after we heard his motivating speech!" —Samuel Woodson, director of marketing.	To sell a high-resistance item (i.e., dating service or time-share condo); to sell an expensive product or service; to reassure recipient.
4. *Identify with*	You know how it is at 6 p.m.—everybody's harried from work, the kids demand attention, it's time to make dinner...	To provoke agreement and gain feeling from recipient that product or service was designed for him or her.

APPROACH	SAMPLE	WHEN TO USE
5. *Ask "What if?"*	What if your boss called you in his office and demoted you—simply because you weren't organized?	To lay groundwork for information to come; to induce recipient to apply the idea to himself or herself and thereby increase your chances for a sale.
6. *Question*	Do you want to save money every time at the dry cleaner—and on every item?	To get recipient to mentally agree and thereby increase your chances of a sale.
7. *State a problem and solution*	The air pollution hovering over our city increases 3% per year...but you can reverse that trend by joining Clear Air Advocates!	To incite action; to create an environment of group action.
8. *Fantasy*	Imagine you and your husband sunning yourselves on the beach at St. Martinique...drinking cool, exotic drinks as you lie on the white sand, the breezes softly caressing your hair...	To sell a pricey product or service; to sell a leisure-time item.
9. *Tell a story*	I announced it: "I'm going to be a famous pianist." They all burst into laughter. I'll show them, I thought.	To sell personal improvement.

ATTENTION-GETTING APPROACHES (Continued)

APPROACH	SAMPLE	WHEN TO USE
10. *Command*	You *cannot ignore* the legislation that your state representative is about to introduce.	When the direct mail message is news; when political or social action is sought; to gain interest for a highly competitive product or service (selling automobiles, for example).
11. *Offer a first*	You are among the first few people in the nation to receive this special offer.	When it is true and important.
12. *Number the ways*	You get four great things when you shop at Food Circus: 1. Low prices 2. Friendly service 3. Super Saver Stamps 4. A chance to win a Jetomatic speedboat!	For highly competitive businesses; to persuade customers who are loyal to a competitor.
13. *Invoke sympathy*	Hungry children cry out in the night. . . you can help with relief through the Concerned and Caring Foster Parents Fund.	To get a response from people who will receive an emotional, rather than tangible, benefit.
14. *Use humor*	"Knock, knock." "Who's there?" "The present Czar." "The present Czar who?" "The present Czar nice, but the cash is better!"	When selling a light-hearted product or service; to establish friendly company reputation.

GET ATTENTION THROUGH THESE 20 APPROACHES

1. Analogy
2. Quote from *Bartlett's Familiar Quotations*
3. Command
4. Develop a paradox
5. Exclusive
6. Fantasy
7. Generic
8. Humor
9. Invitational
10. Juxtapose if/assumptive
11. Kindle amusement
12. Laud a hero
13. Manage identification
14. Numbered ways
15. Offer a first
16. Problem/solution
17. Question
18. Relate a story
19. Satire
20. Testimonial

Used with permission of William Steinhardt, Steinhardt Direct, Shawnee Mission, KS.

A HANDY THESAURUS OF VERBS FOR DIRECT MAIL COPY

When you write direct mail copy, you should repeat your primary message in several different ways. The intent is to sell your product or service effectively. But it is often time-consuming and frustrating to continually try to think of new words.

Some word processing programs have built-in thesauruses, which come in handy for writing copy. Rather than electronically thumbing through lists of words, however, you can always use the following handy guide for finding strong verbs that are useful in writing direct mail copy.

These are grouped into general category for easy use. They are not listed in order of importance.

PERCEIVE

analyze
anticipate
assess
define
determine
discern
evaluate
identify
know
learn
map
measure
pinpoint
rank
rate
read
recognize
review
see
spot
understand

STRONG ACTION

act
affect
assert
boost
build
charge
command
confront
conquer
control
defeat
deliver
demand
direct
empower
express
frame
grow
harness
issue
leverage
master
motivate
negotiate
praise
promote
pull
reduce
sharpen
show
single out
soothe
speed up
spend
spotlight
stop
streamline
supervise
tackle
take charge
thrive
win

ORGANIZE

differentiate
focus
garner
maximize
move
organize
plan
prioritize
save
select

FACILITATE

accommodate
acquire
answer
apply
approach
assure
balance
bridge
claim
coach
communicate
conduct
counsel
deal with
depend
develop
devote
facilitate
freshen
get
handle
implement
inform
involve
join
keep
learn
maintain
manage
polish
prepare
present
redirect
remain
satisfy
segment
situate
sort
stick to
sustain
tap
test
turn
use

ACHIEVE

accept
accomplish
be
convert
create
demonstrate
discover
double
establish
fit
gain
improve
increase
influence
make
multiply
persuade
reach
reduce
resolve
sell
shape
strengthen
triple

"NEGATIVE" ACTION

avoid
break
cancel
change
end
intercept
lose
overcome
regain
sidestep

THE TOP TEN WORDS

When writing your direct mail copy, why not include the ten most powerful words in the English language? According to the psychology department at Yale University, the top ten power words are:

NEW	Human beings continually crave novelty.
SAVE	Everyone wants to save time, energy, or money.
SAFETY	This word indicates long-lasting product quality and relates to personal security.
PROVEN	Documentation works. People like to be persuaded.
LOVE	This word connotes deep inner satisfaction.
DISCOVER	This word stimulates feelings of adventure and excitement.
GUARANTEE	It's what today's consumers demand.
HEALTH	This "new" consciousness will be with us for a long time.
RESULTS	People want to know what will happen, not what it takes to get there.
YOU	This is possibly the most important word of all.

Reprinted with permission, Radio Advertising Bureau's *Sound Management*, 304 Park Avenue South, New York, NY 10010.

THE BIG 96

Here are 96 words commonly found in direct mail copy. Writing direct mail copy isn't like fiction, where originality is valued. In direct mail copy, it is a good idea to use popular words because they are proven sellers. They are listed in alphabetical order.

Actual	Accept	Affect	All
Beautiful	Because	Best	Better
Big	Booklet	Comfortable	Complete
Customer	Deep	Discount	Discover
Dozen	Earn	Easy	Endorsed
Extra	Fast	Fine	Free
Future	Full	Genuine	Get
Gift	Give	Good	Great
Guarantee	Handy	Happy	Heavy
High	Home	Idea	Image
Income	Job	Join	Joy
Keen	Keep	Live	Long
Love	Model	Magic	Many
Men	Natural	Need	News
Offer	Original	Personal	Plan
Practical	Protect	Quality	Real
Receive	Reliable	Sample	Satisfaction
Save	Secret	Send	Smooth
Special	Strong	Sure	Surprising
Take	Thousands	Time	Today
Trial	Under	Unit	Update
Useful	Valid	Value	Vary
Venture	Women	Write	X-Ray
You	Yours	Zip	Zero

Used with permission from William Steinhardt, Steinhardt Direct, Shawnee Mission, KS.

CREATING THE DESIGN

If you're not a designer, don't try to do your own artwork and layout unless it's an extremely simple piece. Find a designer who has done some type of direct mail artwork and, of course, review his or her portfolio.

A designer should provide sketches or a mockup of your piece before beginning production and preparing it for printing. Insist on this intermediary step; it is much cheaper to reject a design before than after production.

Like the copy, the design should fit what you're doing. Here are some ways for you to determine the appropriateness of the design, whether or not you are experienced in art.

Ask yourself if it fits the following elements:

- The type of business
- The type of product or service offered
- The copy
- The price of the product/service offered

Here are some other elements to review in the artwork:

- Does the mood of the piece seem right?
- Does it get attention?
- In a brochure, is there a single focus?
- Is the type appropriate for the artwork and the message?
- Is the type large enough to read? (Many people read direct mail very rapidly, and if they have difficulty reading some parts, they pass them by.)

Where do you find designers, if you don't have recommendations from business associates? Here are several ways:

- Contact the local chapter of the Direct Marketing Association.
- Contact the local IABC (International Association of Business Communicators).
- Contact the local advertising club.
- Check the Yellow Pages under Advertising—Direct Mail, Artists—Commercial, Graphic Designers, or "Desktop Publishing Services."

Put It All Together

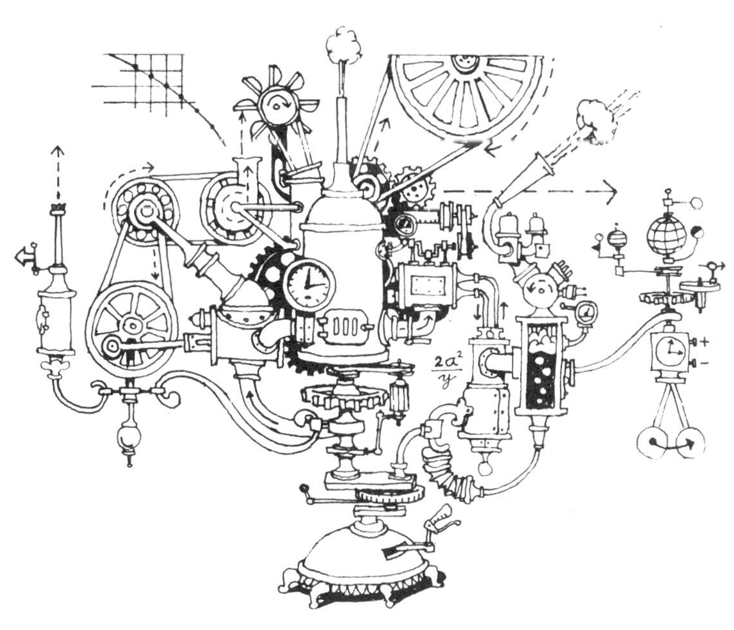

SEPARATING YOUR LISTS FOR TRACKING RESULTS

If you're mailing from more than one list in a single mailing, track returns for each specific list. Let's go back to that earlier example of the entrepreneur in the career consulting business.

Example:

The entrepreneur (career consultant/resume writer) has mailed to three lists:

- Graduates (current year and the past two years) of a local college—394 names
- Subscribers to a local business magazine—12,400 names
- Members of the Advertising and Public Relations Club—692 names

The entrepreneur hand-applied these labels, since the list is small. A label from the first list (graduates) appears like this:

Ms. Susan E. Doe	A
1234 Anystreet Way	
Kansas City, MO 64111	

Because the second list had 12,400 names, she sent this batch to the mailing service. A label from the second list (subscribers) appears like this.

	CAR-RT SORT
Chuck Jones	
4321 Anystreet Place	
Shawnee Mission, KS 66201	

The third list (club members) had labels that were hand-applied, they looked like this:

Bob Wilson	B
1221 Anystreet Lane	
Kansas City, MO 64113	

Our entrepreneur used a response card that had the label on it, mailed in a window envelope. When the results come back, she can identify the first list by the A code in the corner; the third list will have the B code. The list of subscribers was sorted and mailed by carrier route first class, which gave it a special label that is identifiable on its own.

WORKING WITH A PRINTER

Except for very small mailings, you will need a printer to print your mailing pieces. Small mailings—500 or below—can be created on your laser printer, if you have one, but even this might not be the least expensive way to do it.

Here are two tips that will make working with commercial printers more successful:

1. Do not save time on the project by forcing the printer into a rushed deadline. Everybody does this. Plan ahead, put your project into the regular production schedule, and you'll get better results with fewer errors. It doesn't matter that you're the customer—by giving the printer respect and time to print the piece properly, your project will get better treatment.

2. Work with a printer that has produced mailing pieces in the past. These printers understand that they can't substitute a lighter-weight paper at the last minute; or they might recognize that you or your designer has created a piece that violates postal regulations. (The cardinal rule is to *always* check with the post office before printing.)

Get three or more printers to bid, based on your artwork. If you don't have specific needs for paper types, ask the printer what is ''on the floor''—sometimes printers have an overstock of paper from other jobs and you can get it at a lower price. See and feel the paper when you do this, so you'll know what you're getting.

Remember that you don't have to go to one printer for everything. If you're mailing a four-color brochure with a black-and-white letter, you can have the brochure done at one printer, and the letter at another: printers give the best prices for their specialties, and this can save significant amounts of money.

If you haven't picked a particular type of paper or are unfamiliar with what's available, a printer might try to ''sell up'' by convincing you to go with a paper that must be specially ordered, a slick, glossy look, or other expensive alternative. Listen, because he or she might be right. But keep your customers and prospects in mind. You created your package with them in mind and built the project around it. Don't change to enamel (slick) paper when you've designed a simple package.

Do not let the printer and mailing house get at odds with each other. Sometimes a mailing house will receive a printed piece and tell you that the printer did such-and-such wrong and it's going to cost more to imprint the addresses. Choose a mailing house *and* printer before you actually start the work with either. Then, if difficulties arise, you can call back and forth to each as the project progresses.

WORKING WITH A MAILING HOUSE

Mailing services will be required if you need letters stuffed, envelopes sealed, postage applied, and other mechanical aspects of actually getting the printed pieces out. Your best lead is to get recommendations from business associates for mailing houses. If that doesn't turn up anything, check the Yellow Pages under Mailing Services.

Determine ahead of time exactly what needs to be done. Here are some likely choices:

- Envelope-addressing (mag tape or laser) or labeling (by machine or hand)
- Inside-addressing (to personalize a letter, response card, or other piece)
- Folding (letters, brochures, and other applicable pieces)
- Inserting (putting letter, brochure, response card, etc. into envelope)
- Seal envelopes
- Apply postage (stamps by machine or metered)
- Bundle and bag the mailing pieces
- Deliver the mail to the post office

In short, the mailing house does everything that needs to be done to get the pieces in the mail once the printer has printed them.

Your pieces should not have to be sorted by ZIP code. You can acquire the mailing list already arranged that way and whether the mailing house is applying labels or using a mag tape, it's their responsibility to keep it in that order.

Tell the mailing house that you will be available while the project is under way and that you are to be called if anything unusual turns up. This prevents a mailing house from telling you, after the work is complete, that ''The adhesive on the labels wasn't working and they couldn't be applied by machine, so we had to hand-apply them.'' Unfortunately, such situations can occur, and you are supposed to pay higher than the estimated price.

It's best to get a guaranteed bid on the project. This can be done if you have decided on the specifics of number of pieces and work to be done.

Just after you've selected your printer and before you give the printer your artwork, select your mailing house and then tell your contact at the mailing house who your printer is. Then ask, "Is there anything the printer should know before they start the work?"

It's likely the answer is "No." But it might be, "Yes, tell them we can't label such-and-such paper very well on our machines," or some other important specification.

MAILING REGULATIONS

A complete listing of all the regulations and rates related to the U.S. Postal Service could fill this book. Included here is information about the most common areas of concern.

Contact your local post office when planning to do your first direct mail project. In some cities, there is a person who has the title of "mailing requirements clerk." Ask him or her to help you; show a rough sample of the type of mailing piece you would like to do. Don't skip this step—you could incur postage fines or have *all* of your direct mailing returned because you didn't know postal requirements.

DEFINITIONS

Following are basic definitions for each class of mail. Note that most direct mailings go third class. Some, particularly those for small businesses, might go first class or presorted first class.

First-Class Mail

Handwritten or typed letters, post and postal cards, carbon copies, and automatically typed letters and cards. Computer-produced matter is not included unless it has the character of actual and personal correspondence. Also included: bills and statements of account, regardless of preparation method and quantity of identical pieces.

This does not mean that a small business cannot use first-class mail for a direct mailing. If you have a small mailing list of, say, 150 addresses, you would use first-class mail. However, it is unusual for large mailings to go first-class. For mailing rates, see Appendix B.

Presorted first-class mail. A single mailing of 500 or more pieces. Each piece must be part of a group of 10 or more pieces sorted to the same five-digit ZIP code or of a group of 50 or more pieces sort to the same three-digit ZIP code prefix. Each piece must be identical in size and weight, weighing 11 oz. or less. Pieces that do not meet these requirements incur a regular first-class mail charge.

Carrier route first-class mail. A single mailing of 500 or more pieces, like presorted first-class mail, but sorted down to the carrier route. This provides an even less expensive mailing rate. The weight and size requirements are the same as for presorted first-class mail.

Some of this information is reprinted from *Mail Management Manual*, published by Tension Envelope Corporation, Kansas City, Missouri. Used with permission from publisher.

Second-Class Mail

Includes newspapers and periodicals regularly issued from a known office at stated intervals of at least four times per year and bearing notice of entry as second-class matter.

Special presorting and packaging is required. Check with your post office.

Third-Class Mail

Circulars, form letters, books, catalogs, and merchandise such as seeds, bulbs, cuttings, photographs, drawings, keys, etc. Must weight less than 16 ounces. Special rates are given to qualifying nonprofit organizations. Since this is the most common direct mailing method, detailed postal information is provided in Appendix A at the end of this book. For third-class mailing rates, see Appendix B.

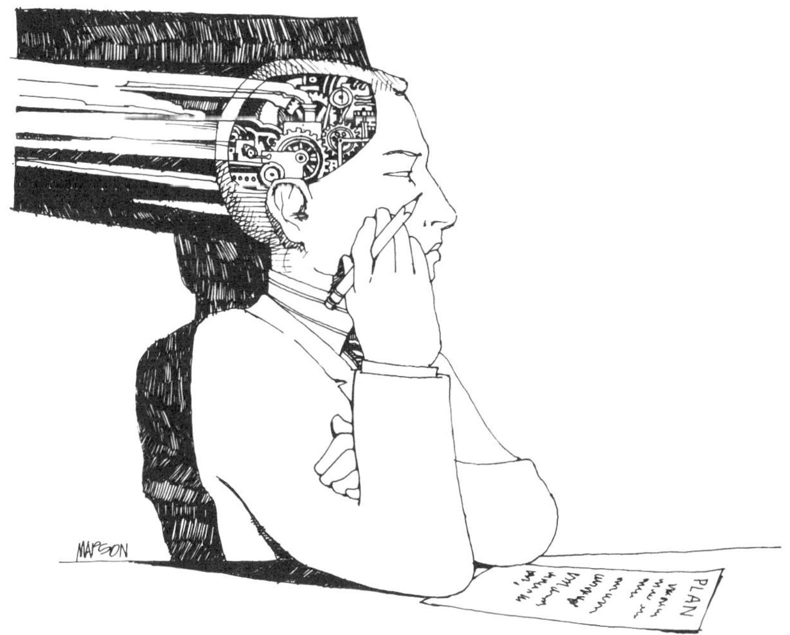

MAILING REGULATIONS (Continued)

Fourth-Class Mail

Mailable matter weighing 16 ounces or more that is not included in first, second, or third class. These include:

Parcel post. Mailings of minimum 300 pieces or 2,000 pounds. Parcels need not be identical size or content.

Bound printed matter. Weighs at least one pound and not more than 10 pounds. Advertising, promotional, directory, or editorial matter securely bound by permanent fastenings (this does not include looseleaf binders). Bulk mailings in this class requires 300+ pieces that are identical in weight and size.

Special fourth-class rate. Primarily books, films, music-related materials, sound recordings, scripts, looseleaf binders, and computer-readable media. Check with the post office for specifics.

Fourth-class library rate. Materials in paragraph above and selected additional materials exchanged between schools, libraries, nonprofit organizations, and other groups. Check with the post office for specifics.

Business Reply Mail

Business reply envelopes, cards, cartons, and labels distributed by mailers for return with prepayment of postage.

Mailing rates. Mailing rates are based on weight. See Appendix B.

Size Standards
Domestic (Letter) Mail

Thickness: .007 inch minimum
Shape: Rectangular (round, triangle, etc., not acceptable)
Height: 3½″ minimum
Length: 5″ minimum

Postcards

Thickness: .007 inch minimum; .0095 inch maximum
(Not sure? Many post offices actually have a device that can measure this.)
Shape: Rectangular. Height to width ratio must be between 1:1.3 and 1:2.5
Height minimum: 3½ inches — *Length minimum:* 5 inches
Height maximum: 4¼ inches — *Length maximum:* 6 inches

Nonstandard Mail

Nonstandard mail is first-class mail (except for presort first-class and carrier route first-class) or single-piece-rate third-class mail, weighing one ounce or less, that exceeds any of these dimensions:

Length: 11½″
Height: 6⅛″
Thickness: ¼″
Proportion: When the length divided by the height is not between 1.3 and 2.5 exclusive, it is a nonstandard mailing piece.

These kinds of nonstandard mail are subject to a surcharge of $.10 each, in addition to applicable postage and fees. Presort first-class and carrier route first-class that is nonstandard has a surcharge of $.05.

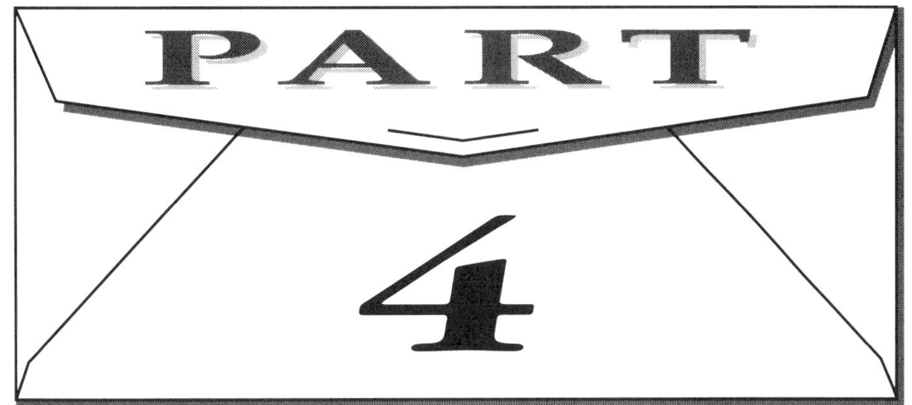

Results Make The Difference

HOW TO COMPILE YOUR OWN LIST

Perhaps you haven't yet created a mailing list of your current customers or prospects. Begin doing so immediately. Here are other ways to develop a list. Check Yes or No to indicate whether these sources are useful to you.

YES	NO	Source
___	___	Sign-up sheet in your store
___	___	Members of professional organizations
___	___	Members of service organizations
___	___	Names from your sales staff
___	___	Newspaper listings—births, weddings, engagements
___	___	Newspaper listings—job promotions or awards
___	___	Telephone directories and city directories (in the latter, you can review listings by area for specific neighborhoods)
___	___	Permits (building, remodeling, repairs, etc.)

Think up a few of your own:

___ ___ ____

___ ___ ____

___ ___ ____

___ ___ ____

It might be tedious, but a few names here and a few names there, and it adds up. You may also have a valuable item to rent—your own mailing list.

IN HOUSE LIST (Continued)

But Should I?

It seems natural to question renting out your in-house list. After all, it's one of your most valuable resources. However, you might as well, because the names on your list are already on other lists in various ways, and other people are making money on those lists.

You don't have to rent your list to competitors, although in many industries this is common. On a local or regional basis, it might not be wise.

Be sure to ''seed'' your list before you do rent it. Add several decoy names and some real but undetectable addresses. You could use a post office box or use your home address. You can use a secretary's name and fictitious apartment number with your company address (if it isn't instantly recognizable as your business address). Change these decoys periodically.

Your Goldmine List

Don't create your own list just to rent it out. Offer new products and services to your in-house mailing list on a regular basis. That's the best direct mail program you'll find.

MEASURING YOUR RESULTS

Once your mailing has been done and you've handled the results (hosting your open house, having salespeople follow the leads, etc.), don't assume the project is over. It's time to assess the results of the mailing. This is the only way to ensure that your direct mail programs get more and more efficient.

How do you compare the cost of a mailing program to 5,000 people to a piece that was mailed to 40,000? Also, isn't it comparing apples and oranges to measure a four-color piece against a black-and-white one? Not really. There is a standard equation you can use to measure your results:

Promotion costs ÷ Number of Responses = Cost Per Response (CPR)

If you have one highly successful mailing and have the budget to try again, do so. Many businesses have learned that direct mail works like science. The response you receive from a list predictably returns similar results during future mailings. Review the steps as listed in this book, and constantly network for tips from other business associates who use direct mail. (An excellent book on networking is Crisp Publications' *Effective Networking*. See the order form in the back of this book.)

HOW OFTEN DO I MAIL IN THE FUTURE?

If you've decided that direct mail is a regular part of your business, you might wonder how often to mail. Because businesses and products are so different, you will need to experiment to learn what works best for you. Following are some options for you to consider. You might do:

- a periodic mailing (every month or six weeks) with a different offer each time.
- four mailings a year, tied to the specific seasons.
- frequent mailings in the season in which you need the most business. (This is where timeframe is important.)
- staggered mailings to various lists. This is particularly handy if salespeople must personally handle each response card by calling on the customer. An example would be acquiring a list of 10,000 and then mailing 2,000 pieces per time, with each mailing two weeks apart.

Write your own ideas:

- ____________________
  ____
  ____
- ____________________
  ____
  ____
- ____________________
  ____
  ____
- ____________________
  ____
  ____

GO FOR IT!

Once you've measured your results and demonstrated that direct mail can improve your business and your profitability, you may wonder how you got along without it. May direct mail work so well for you that it's like magic!

APPENDIX A: POSTAL REGULATIONS FOR THIRD CLASS MAIL

Definitions of Third-Class Matter:

GENERAL	Mailable matter (1) weighing less than 16 ounces, (2) not required to be mailed first-class, and (3) not entered as second-class mail.
CIRCULARS/ FORM LETTERS	Besides printed message, contain only written, handwritten, or hand-stamped dates of writing; name and address of person addressed and of sender; a stamped or written serial number; and corrections of mere typographical errors.
BOOKS/ CATALOGS	Contain 24 or more bound pages, with at least 22 pages printed, and weighing less than 16 ounces.
MERCHANDISE	Seeds, bulbs, cuttings, roots, plants, photographs, drawings, keys, etc.
PROOF SHEET CORRECTIONS	Include alteration of text and insertion of new matter, as marginal instructions to printer.

Applications of Third-Class Rates/Methods

SINGLE RATE	Applied to each piece according to weight.
BULK RATE	Applied to mailings of identical pieces, separately addressed, in quantities not less than 50 pounds or less than 200 pieces. All pieces must be identical in size, weight, and number of enclosures if paid by permit imprint but textural matter need not be identical. Postage computed at pound rates on entire bulk mailed at one time.
CARRIER ROUTE PRE-SORT	Similar to bulk rate, except minimum number of pieces is 200, and must be presorted with 10 or more pieces packaged to the same carrier delivery route and appropriately marked.
KEYS AND IDENTIFICATION ITEMS	Applied to each item according to weight.
SPECIAL RATES	Applied to qualifying nonprofit organizations.

Permits and Fee for Mailers

Annual fee must be paid by or for anyone who mails at bulk third-class rates. The fee is separate from permit imprint fee (paid only once and nonrecurring).

Postage Payment/Required Markings for Third-Class Mail

POSTAGE PREPAID BY:	Permit Imprint  Meter Stamp  Precanceled Stamps 
MARKINGS REQUIRED:	Identifying words printed or rubber stamped either in or adjacent to postage: • Bulk Rate or Blk. Rt. • Carrier Route or CAR-RT • Nonprofit Organization or Nonprofit Org.

Weight and Size Limits

MAXIMUM WEIGHT:	Each piece less than 16 ounces
MAXIMUM SIZE:	11¾″×14″ (Single-piece third-class under 2 oz., and more than 6⅛″ high or 11½″ wide or ¼″ thick must pay $.10 surcharge)
SHAPE:	Standards for envelopes, cards, and self-mailers with postage paid at third-class rate: • Pieces less than 3½″ in height or 5 inches in length, or .007″ in thickness are unmailable. • Single-piece third-class pieces under 2 oz., with height to width ratio not between 1:1.3 and 1:2.5, must pay $.10 surcharge. • Pieces not sealed or secured on all four edges so that they may be handled by machines are not recommended.

Preparation of Third-Class Mail and Statements

Mailers must sort, face, and tie bulk mail into packages both lengthwise and crosswise with twine strong enough to withstand handling in the mail. Rubber bands may also be used if they meet specifications. Total weight of pieces in one sack not to exceed 70 pounds. Use package labels (and facing slips on mixed state and foreign packages), on lower left corner of top piece on letter size packages; next to address on larger packages.

Mailer's statement must be submitted with each mailing as follows:

- Statement of Mailing Matters with Permit Imprints (Form 3602) for mail with permit imprints.
- Bulk Rate Mailing Statement—Third-Class Mail (Form 3602-PC) for mail bearing precanceled stamps or meter stamps.

Packages to be prepared by mailer as follows:

- Five-digit packages and sacks:
  1. When there are 10 or more individually addressed pieces to the same five-digit zip code delivery unit, face pieces in same direction and securely wrap or tie together as a package. Label not required, but red label D recommended. Five-digit sacks must contain a minimum of 125 pieces or 15 pounds of mail. Sacks may contain no more than 70 pounds of mail.
  2. Identify sack contents as third-class (3C) and as LETTER or FLAT. Flats are mailing pieces larger than 6⅛″ × 11½.″
  3. Label five-digit sacks:
     Sample:

        PHILADELPHIA PA 19118
        3C LTRS
        BOSTON MA 021

- Three-digit packages and sacks:
  1. When there are 10 or more pieces for the same three-digit ZIP code, after all five-digit packages have been made, mailers must make up three-digit packages and affix a green label three to each package.
  2. A three-digit sack must be labeled in the following manner:
     Line 1: City, state, three-digit prefix
     Line 2: Contents
     Line 3: Office of mailing
     Sample:

        PHILADELPHIA PA 191
        3C LTRS
        BOSTON MA 021

  3. Three-digit sacks must contain a minimum of 125 pieces of mail or 15 pounds.

POSTAL REGULATIONS (Continued)

- State packages and sacks:
  1. Pieces remaining for a state must be combined in a state package and labeled with orange label S.
  2. Sacks containing state packages, must be labeled:

     DIS KANSAS CITY MO 640
     3C LTRS MO
     SAN FRANCISCO 941

  3. State sacks containing fewer than 125 pieces of mail or/and less than 15 pounds may be prepared.

- Mixed states packages and sacks:
  1. All pieces remaining after the above packages have been prepared must be combined in a mixed states package and labeled with a tan mixed state label.
  2. Sacks containing mixed states packages must be addressed to the state distribution center and labeled:

     MXD KANSAS CITY MO 640
     3C LTRS MXD STATES
     KANSAS CITY MO 640

  3. A mixed state sack label contains the following:
     Line 1: Distribution point
     Line 2: Contents followed by ''MXD STATES''
     Line 3: Point of origin

Sealing/Marking

Examination. Prepare third-class mail to be easily examined (postal inspection is permitted on third-class). Third-class mail not sealed or secured so that it may be handled by machines is not recommended.

Marking. Sealed pieces mailed at single-piece third-class postage rate must be legibly marked, preferably below postage and above name of addressee, with two words: **Third-Class**. Markings may be included as part of permit imprint, and may be printed adjacent to meter stamp by postage meter. Not necessary to use endorsement ''Third Class'' on sealed matter at bulk third-class rates. Bulk rate endorsement will suffice.

ZIP Coding Requirements

To take advantage of second and third-class bulk mailing rates you must ZIP code and presort to ZIP code numbers.

Regulations:

- Address on each piece must include ZIP code except that it may be omitted from pieces:
    1. Bearing a simplified address: Postal Customer, Householder, Resident.
    2. Presorted and bundled by mailer to city, rural, or contract carrier routes.
    3. Presorted to five-digit ZIP code destinations consisting of either a post office having one ZIP code or the ZIP code postal zone in multi–ZIP coded post offices.

- Presorting requires mailers to make additional sorting, bundling, and sacking by all five ZIP code digits.

Merchandise Samples

When an article given away for the purpose of advertising merchandise is mailed at bulk third-class rates for general distribution on city delivery routes—in a mailing piece exceeding 5″ in width or ¼″ thickness (or which has non-uniformity in thickness), the mailer must comply with special preparation requirements. Inquire at a post office.

Urgent Envelopes

Third-class envelopes bearing references to expedited handling such as Rush, Express, Overnight, must be prepared as follows:

- Words "Bulk Rate" or "Nonprofit Org." displayed more prominently than any other words in the permit imprint.
- Leave ⅜″ clear space around the permit.

Identification of Nonprofit Mail

Nonprofit third-class mail must contain the name and return address of the authorized nonprofit organization. This identification must appear either on the outside of the mailing piece or in a prominent location on the enclosure.

NOTES

FOR OTHER FIFTY-MINUTE SELF-STUDY BOOKS
SEE THE BACK OF THIS BOOK.

NOTES

FOR OTHER FIFTY-MINUTE SELF-STUDY BOOKS
SEE THE BACK OF THIS BOOK.

NOTES

FOR OTHER FIFTY-MINUTE SELF-STUDY BOOKS
SEE THE BACK OF THIS BOOK.

NOTES

FOR OTHER FIFTY-MINUTE SELF-STUDY BOOKS
SEE THE BACK OF THIS BOOK.

NOTES

FOR OTHER FIFTY-MINUTE SELF-STUDY BOOKS
SEE THE BACK OF THIS BOOK.

ABOUT THE FIFTY-MINUTE SERIES

We hope you enjoyed this book and found it valuable. If so, we have good news for you. This title is part of the best selling ***FIFTY-MINUTE Series*** of books. All ***Series*** books are similar in size and format, and identical in price. Several are supported with training videos. These are identified by the symbol Ⓥ next to the title.

Since the first ***FIFTY-MINUTE*** book appeared in 1986, millions of copies have been sold worldwide. Each book was developed with the reader in mind. The result is a concise, high quality module written in a positive, readable self-study format.

FIFTY-MINUTE Books and Videos are available from your distributor. A free current catalog is available on request from Crisp Publications, Inc., 95 First Street, Los Altos, CA 94022.

Following is a complete list of ***FIFTY-MINUTE Series*** Books and Videos organized by general subject area.

Management Training:

Ⓥ	Coaching & Counseling	68-8
	Delegating for Results	008-6
	Developing Instructional Design	076-0
Ⓥ	Effective Meeting Skills	33-5
Ⓥ	Empowerment	096-5
	Ethics in Business	69-6
Ⓥ	An Honest Day's Work: Motivating Employees	39-4
Ⓥ	Increasing Employee Productivity	10-8
Ⓥ	Leadership Skills for Women	62-9
	Learning To Lead	43-4
Ⓥ	Managing Disagreement Constructively	41-6
Ⓥ	Managing for Commitment	099-X
Ⓥ	Managing Organizational Change	80-7
	Mentoring	123-6
Ⓥ	The New Supervisor — Revised	120-1
	Personal Performance Contracts — Revised	12-2
Ⓥ	Project Management	75-0
Ⓥ	Quality at Work: A Personal Guide to Professional Standards	72-6
	Rate Your Skills as a Manager	101-5
	Recruiting Volunteers in Non-Profit Organizations	141-4
	Risk Taking	076-9

Management Training (continued):

	Title	No.
	Selecting & Working With Consultants	87-4
	Self-Managing Teams	00-0
V	Successful Negotiation — Revised	09-2
	Systematic Problem-Solving & Decision-Making	63-7
V	Team Building — Revised	118-X
	Training Managers to Train	43-2
	Training Methods that Work	082-5
	Understanding Organizational Change	71-8
V	Working Together in a Multi-Cultural Organization	85-8

Personal Improvement:

	Title	No.
V	Attitude: Your Most Priceless Possession — Revised	011-6
	Business Etiquette & Professionalism	32-9
	Concentration!	073-6
	The Continuously Improving Self: A Personal Guide to TQM	151-1
V	Developing Positive Assertiveness	38-6
	Developing Self-Esteem	66-1
	Finding Your Purpose: A Guide to Personal Fulfillment	072-8
	Managing Anger	114-7
	Memory Skills in Business	56-4
	Organizing Your Workspace	125-2
V	Personal Time Management	22-X
	Plan Your Work—Work Your Plan!	078-7
	Self-Empowerment	128-7
	Stop Procrastinating: Get To Work!	88-2
	Successful Self-Management	26-2
	The Telephone & Time Management	53-X
	Twelve Steps to Self-Improvement	102-3

Human Resources & Wellness:

	Title	No.
	Attacking Absenteeism	042-6
V	Balancing Home & Career — Revised	35-3
	Downsizing Without Disaster	081-7
	Effective Performance Appraisals — Revised	11-4
	Effective Recruiting Strategies	127-9
	Employee Benefits with Cost Control	133-3
	Giving & Receiving Criticism	023-X
	Guide to Affirmative Action	54-8
	Health Strategies for Working Women	079-5
V	High Performance Hiring	088-4
V	Job Performance & Chemical Dependency	27-0
V	Managing Personal Change	74-2
	Managing Upward: Managing Your Boss	131-7
V	Men and Women: Partners at Work	009-4
V	Mental Fitness: A Guide to Stress Management	15-7
	New Employee Orientation	46-7
	Office Management: A Guide to Productivity	005-1
	Overcoming Anxiety	29-9

Human Resources & Wellness (continued):

	Title	No.
	Personal Counseling	14-9
	Personal Wellness: Achieving Balance for Healthy Living	21-3
	Preventing Job Burnout	23-8
	Productivity at the Workstation: Wellness & Fitness at Your Desk	41-8
	Professional Excellence for Secretaries	52-1
	Quality Interviewing — Revised	13-0
	Sexual Harassment in the Workplace	153-8
	Stress that Motivates: Self-Talk Secrets for Success	150-3
	Wellness in the Workplace	020-5
	Winning at Human Relations	86-6
	Writing a Human Resources Manual	70-X
V	Your First Thirty Days in a New Job	003-5

Communications & Creativity:

	Title	No.
	The Art of Communicating	45-9
V	Better Business Writing — Revised	25-4
V	The Business of Listening	34-3
	Business Report Writing	122-8
	Creative Decision Making	098-1
V	Creativity in Business	67-X
	Dealing Effectively with the Media	116-3
V	Effective Presentation Skills	24-6
	Fifty One-Minute Tips to Better Communication	071-X
	Formatting Letters & Memos on the Microcomputer	130-9
	Influencing Others	84-X
V	Making Humor Work	61-0
	Speedreading in Business	78-5
	Technical Presentation Skills	55-6
	Technical Writing in the Corporate World	004-3
	Thinking on Your Feet	117-1
	Visual Aids in Business	77-7
	Writing Fitness	35-1

Customer Service/Sales Training:

	Title	No.
	Beyond Customer Service: The Art of Customer Retention	115-5
V	Calming Upset Customers	65-3
V	Customer Satisfaction — Revised	84-1
	Effective Sales Management	31-0
	Exhibiting at Tradeshows	137-6
	Improving Your Company Image	136-8
	Managing Quality Customer Service	83-1
	Professional Selling	42-4
V	Quality Customer Service — Revised	95-5
	Restaurant Server's Guide — Revised	08-4
	Sales Training Basics — Revised	119-8
	Telemarketing Basics	60-2
V	Telephone Courtesy & Customer Service — Revised	64-7

Small Business & Financial Planning:

The Accounting Cycle	146-5
The Basics of Budgeting	134-1
Consulting for Success	006-X
Credits & Collections	080-9
Direct Mail Magic	075-2
Financial Analysis: Beyond the Basics	132-5
Financial Planning With Employee Benefits	90-4
Marketing Your Consulting or Professional Services	40-8
Personal Financial Fitness — Revised	89-0
Publicity Power	82-3
Starting Your New Business — Revised	144-9
Understanding Financial Statements	22-1
Writing & Implementing Your Marketing Plan	083-3

Adult Literacy & Learning:

Basic Business Math	24-8
Becoming an Effective Tutor	28-0
Building Blocks of Business Writing	095-7
Clear Writing	094-9
The College Experience: Your First Thirty Days on Campus	07-8
Going Back to School: An Adult Perspective	142-2
Introduction to Microcomputers: The Least You Should Know	087-6
Language, Customs & Protocol For Foreign Students	097-3
Reading Improvement	086-8
Returning to Learning: Getting Your G.E.D.	02-7
Study Skills Strategies — Revised	05-X
Vocabulary Improvement	124-4

Career/Retirement & Life Planning:

Career Discovery — Revised	07-6
Developing Strategic Resumes	129-5
Effective Networking	30-2
I Got The Job! — Revised	121-X
Job Search That Works	105-8
Plan B: Protecting Your Career from Change	48-3
Preparing for Your Interview	33-7